FUND-RAISING PROJECTS

With a World Hunger Emphasis

Paul Longacre

Illustrated by James Converse

HERALD PRESS
Scottdale, Pennsylvania
Kitchener, Ontario
1980

FUND-RAISING PROJECTS WITH A WORLD
  HUNGER EMPHASIS
Copyright © 1980 by Herald Press, Scottdale, Pa. 15683
  Published simultaneously in Canada by Herald Press,
  Kitchener, Ont. N2G 4M5
Library of Congress Catalog Card Number: 80-83771
International Standard Book Number: 0-8361-1940-1
Printed in the United States of America
Design: Alice B. Shetler

15 14 13 12 11 10 9 8 7 6 5 4 3 2 1

Contents

Author's Preface

This booklet began to take shape in response to a pastor's letter requesting ideas his youth group could use to raise money for Mennonite Central Committee's relief and development program. I scoured several resources on world hunger and found no ideas for fund-raising projects.

The pages which follow describe some traditional fund-raising projects. But many other projects have been included because of the growing concern about the large energy and food waste in Canada and the United States. The suggested projects can help us experience the joy and satisfaction of helping needy people while gaining some freedom over our wasteful habits.

Rather than simply outlining fund-raising projects, I attempted to describe some of the causes of world hunger and link specific projects to these causes. Often the best climate for learning is when persons are engaged in specific related activities.

I am indebted to a number of persons for ideas and help in preparing this booklet. Suggestions from colleagues at the Mennonite Central Committee office were helpful. Mark Kelley's editing was much needed. Faith Hershberger's typing and research skills were invaluable. My late wife, Doris's, ideas and encouragement were constant and essential.

I hope and pray that this booklet will provide a lot of fun and new understanding along with significant earnings.

Paul Longacre
Hunger Concerns Secretary
Mennonite Central Committee (MCC)
Akron, Pennsylvania

Introduction

Many North Americans wish someone would invent a simple, effective way to solve the world hunger problem. We want a miracle mush, inexpensive, easy to ship and distribute, readily accepted by starving people, and a product which eliminates the problem without affecting the way *we* live. Unfortunately, there is no easy way out of the world food crisis.

The problem has many sides—political, economic, social, psychological, and even spiritual. After more than thirty years of work by governments, voluntary agencies, and church groups, a solution still seems impossible or at least very difficult. In fact, instead of going away, the world hunger situation is growing more complex. What can we do?

This book suggests 21 projects through which you, your family, or your group can raise money to support development programs which help the hungry. Each project is designed also to help you discover more about problems here at home, such as food waste and excessive use of petroleum products, electricity, and other natural resources which contribute to the hunger problems in other countries.

Claiming we don't know any hungry people will not get us off the hook, according to Jesus' words in Matthew 25. The exclamation, "Lord, when did we see thee hungry or thirsty . . . ?" was not an adequate excuse. Learning about the hunger problem and responding to needs go together.

Finding all the causes of hunger will take much more time. But we can't wait until we know the whole story to act. We may make mistakes, but hopefully our small steps now will lead to more important steps in the future. As you work on projects to help the poor, you can discover how our affluent Western lifestyle often helps keep people poor. The ideas in this book remind us what a gigantic demand our wasteful habits make on the world's limited resources. Out of this simple process may come more productive ways of responding to the dilemma.

Tied to the instructions for each project is a brief explanation of a related aspect of the hunger problem. If you want to explore any of these factors in greater detail, the books and audiovisual materials listed on pages 68 and 69 and the agencies listed on page 70 will provide more information.

Most of these projects require only minimal effort and expense. Some of them are good substitutes for more expensive entertainment. Tasks like gleaning corn or a hunger walk can be monotonous if you do them alone, but if you try them as a group, you can have a lot of fun. Children, youth, and adults can join together for a creative, enjoyable experience.

The projects only illustrate the many different activities you can initiate to raise money for world hunger. Innovate and create your own fund-raising projects, using the 21 projects in this booklet as idea starters. Also think up creative activities and projects that reduce waste and help the hungry even though they don't raise any money.

When your project is completed, you face another important responsibility. Where will you donate the money? Denominational groups will likely want to contribute to programs run by their own churches. For example, Mennonites will likely give to Mennonite Central Committee, Lutherans to Lutheran World Relief, Catholics to Catholic Relief Service, and United Methodists to United Methodist Committee for Overseas Relief, Church World Service, or CROP.

Keep in mind that people need the food and other basic necessities relief agencies provide. But development programs work at solving the root causes of hunger and poverty by helping people improve their employment and food growing

10

potential. Carefully consider the available programs before you give your money.

Christians who work face-to-face with the hunger problem today say we must do three things to help those in need: (1) expand our aid to poor countries, (2) cut back our own excessive consumption of the world's precious resources, and (3) press for more equal distribution of these available resources. North Americans, 6 percent of the world's population, use 30 to 40 percent of the earth's resources. The average North American gobbles up four times as many food resources as does someone living in Southern Asia. That doesn't leave much for the rest of the world.

The 21 projects in this booklet, linking fund-raising ideas to the complex realities of world hunger, are intended to encourage you, your family, or your group to work at giving more to those in need while reducing the amount you keep for yourself.

FUND-RAISING
PROJECTS
With a World Hunger Emphasis

1
Crop Gleaning

The Project

Survival for many Old Testament people depended at least in part on gleaning—gathering the remnants of the harvest left in the fields and vineyards by the farmers. In the Book of Ruth in the Bible, Ruth might never have met Boaz if he had not observed the custom of leaving the corners of his fields unreaped. Your gleaning project may not seem as dramatic as that, but it will save produce which might otherwise be wasted and it provides a simple way to raise money for relief and development programs.

Fruits, nuts, corn, potatoes, and other vegetables are all crops from which some of the harvest is left behind on the ground or in the tree. The kind of produce you find will depend on your geographical location. Survey your community to discover which crops result in the most waste and where you are most likely to make a profit from your efforts. If storms and wet weather strike at harvesttime, commercial pickers may do a less thorough job, resulting in a more abundant leftover harvest for you.

Two essential points to keep in mind as you plan to glean are: (1) Be sure to get permission from landowners or crop producers before you start picking up the leftovers. (2) Make arrangements to sell your harvest. Be careful not to compete with the producer who allows you to work in his field.

Try to ensure that your gleaning will produce a modest return in produce and income. If your group members spend half a day bent over in a cornfield or dangling from ladders in a cherry orchard, they want to earn more than a dollar per worker. Getting *enough* workers should be easy since almost anyone can participate. And you need little if any special equipment.

If you can't find field work, try getting the fruit or vegetables rejected by a local packing house. You might be able to arrange with the owners to haul these culls away at little or no cost. Resort and sell them. A California fruit grower set up a culled fruit stand with a payment box marked "Proceeds for MCC World Hunger." He trusted customers to serve themselves and drop the money in the box. Many customers paid more than the prices marked on the fruit.

What's the Connection?

Food waste is a serious problem in North America and in the poor countries of the world. Here at home crop loss in storage ranges from five to 10 percent. Less developed nations, where tropical heat and humidity create more difficult conditions, lose as much as a quarter of the harvest. One Mennonite Central

Committee administrator observed over 1,000 sacks of maize (corn) rotting in Zambia because there were no trucks to pick it up before the rains started. Often diseases, insects, and pests claim one third of the crop's value before it even reaches storage facilities.[1]

Poor people battle constantly to preserve their limited food stores, while Americans and Canadians luxuriate in a practice people in less-developed countries probably can't imagine. Reports show that once it reaches the market, we throw away 10 percent of our food. That amounts to a 13.7-million-ton pile for the U.S. every year.[2] To haul just a million tons of wheat takes 11,000 railroad hopper cars, so you can see why garbage collectors are seldom found on the lists of the unemployed.

2
Nut Gathering

The Project

Many North American nut trees go unharvested every year, resulting in the loss of a valuable food resource. Common varieties such as black walnut, pecan, hickory (or shell barks), and English walnuts can be located readily in wood lots, along roadsides, or on the grounds of old homesteads. One fall my daughters and I gathered black walnuts at a nearby historical site. A simple conversation with the caretaker provided us with the necessary permission to collect the nuts. We picked up several bushels of the larger nuts from twenty trees.

After you gather the nuts, you will need to hull and dry them. Black and English walnut meat blackens and can become unusable if the nut isn't separated from the green outer hull. A simple hulling method for black or hickory nuts is to spread them on a well-traveled, *unpaved* driveway. The vehicle tires will grind away the hulls with only minimal cracking of the nuts. Once the hulls are off, you can separate the good nuts from the undeveloped ones by dumping the whole batch into a bucket of water; the bad ones float.

Cracking the nuts poses another challenge. Many people use a hammer, but several inexpensive nutcrackers are available. For hard-to-crack black walnuts, the commercial crackers are especially helpful. Soaking black walnuts for 12 to 18 hours before you attack them helps, too. You can sell your harvest through a local food market, food co-ops, natural food stores, classified ads in your newspaper, or through orders from friends and neighbors. Cracked nuts are in high demand, particularly during the November and December Christmas baking season.

What's the Connection?

Using nuts that would normally go to waste won't do much to correct the protein shortage which exists in certain parts of the world, but it can help us realize the imbalance of protein consumption between the West and the poor countries. Some economically disadvantaged nations tie up many acres of their land raising nuts for export to affluent countries. For instance, groundnuts (peanuts) produced in Sub-Sahara Africa are a major ingredient in European animal feeds.

You may be shocked to learn that our part of the world imports more protein from poor countries than we ship to them. In other words, there is more protein in the oil seeds, fish meal, beef, and other foods we receive from poor nations than there is in the grain we send to them. In effect, the rich nations of the West are depriving millions of people in tropical Africa, Latin America, and Asia of protein essential to their diet.

3

Wood Gathering

The Project

Rising oil, gas, and electricity costs have caused many people to consider using wood-burning stoves and fireplaces for home heating. According to the Fireplace Institute, 65 percent of all new single family homes have fireplaces. In addition, wood stove sales have increased sevenfold since 1972. Your group can capitalize on this new energy consciousness to raise money and help reduce oil and gas consumption.

Finding wood should be fairly easy. Some of your church members or relatives may have woodlots where you can gather an ample supply. Look around your community for fencerows or dead trees in pastures. Builders often burn or bury scrap wood from construction sites which you could salvage and sell.

Industrial plants frequently discard packing crates, broken pallets, and other scrap wood which you can haul away. Tree service companies and nurseries might be looking for ways to dispose of wood they cut. Be sure to ask before you take anything away.

With a little more effort, you can cut wood in local municipal watersheds and state or federally owned forests. Contact the U.S. Forest Service or your local extension office for information on local, state, and federal forests near you and the kind of permit required for wood gathering. In Pennsylvania, for instance, a $3.00 permit allows you to remove a cord (128 cubic feet) of wood from state forests. In Ontario a $7.00 permit will allow you to cut a cord of wood from forests managed by the Ministry of Natural Resources. A cord will more than fill the back of a pickup truck.

Dry wood can be sold immediately. But if you cut green stuff, stack it and wait a year until it's ready. Try to cut hard woods like oak, maple, and fruit tree wood as much as possible. They top the list of home heating woods. Several books and pamphlets are available which list various woods and their heat content. Remember, the harder the wood the more it's worth.

You can sell the wood two ways:

(1) Directly through classified newpaper ads and orders taken through church or civic groups.

(2) Wholesale through grocery and hardware stores or roadside markets.

A word of caution. There's a lot more to cutting trees than yelling "Timber!" If you're planning to use power equipment, be sure an experienced adult or older youth is part of the group. And always know which way you're going to run when the tree falls. Trees may look graceful and light when they're standing, but they pack a tremendous punch when they crash to the ground.

21

What's the Connection?

Heating and cooling the space inside a typical North American house uses up about 65 percent of the total household energy budget.[3] Burning wood reduces the heating cost and helps conserve the earth's diminishing oil and gas supply.

Rising oil prices, which have spurred the renewed interest in wood heat, have affected one half of North America much more than the other. The United States depends on costly foreign oil for about half of its total supply, while Canada stands nearly self-sufficient in petroleum production though imported oil is used in the eastern provinces. Regardless of source, however, North Americans as a whole use more than twice as much energy per person as people living in the industrialized countries of Europe and more than 10 times as much as residents of the poorer Asian and African nations.[4]

4
Recycling

The Project

Foreigners visiting America for the first time often are shocked at the amount of material we throw away. That includes Europeans, who share our standard of living, as well as visitors from poor countries. Our throw-away mentality costs us about four billion dollars a year in collection and disposal fees. In many cities, waste management expenses rank second only to education.[5] Recycling some of the materials we discard (aluminum, steel, copper, paper, and glass) can help reduce our massive waste and earn money.

The first step in planning a recycling project is to find out where you can sell various reusable materials, what conditions are involved, the minimum amount you can deliver, and which materials return the greatest profit. Some communities don't have outlets for certain metal and paper products. You can avoid a lot of headaches and improve your profits if you check out all the details before your group has piled up three tons of bottle caps that cannot be recycled.

Payment for materials fluctuates. Currently, in eastern Pennsylvania, delivering a pound of aluminum will earn you 20¢, 100 pounds of newsprint brings 30¢, 100 pounds of corrugated cardboard returns $1.25, and 100 pounds of white office paper will bring $3.00. In one area, however, the rate for a ton of newsprint bounced between a high of $60 per ton and a low of $12 per ton in a period of several years.

Two organizations which have been involved in recycling for some time have prepared information packets for groups interested in starting a project. You can write to: Earth Keepers, c/o Eastern Mennonite College, Harrisonburg, Va. 22801; or MCC (Ontario), 50 Kent Avenue, Kitchener, Ont. N2G 3R1.

What's the Connection?

Recycling not only raises funds for world hunger but also conserves resources and protects the environment. One expert says significant amounts of materials could be salvaged if everyone helped just a little. According to Denis Hayes of the Worldwatch Institute, "At least two-thirds of the material resources that we now waste could be reused without important changes in our lifestyles."[6]

Reusing waste material conserves energy, too. Recycling newsprint saves 23 percent of the energy required to produce it from new materials.[7] Reusing steel saves 47 percent of the energy required to make it, and aluminum recycling saves a full 95 percent of the energy involved in production.[8]

Many of the mineral resources used in the United States

come from other countries. For example, the U.S. depends on foreign sources for 84 percent of its aluminum and tin, 29 percent of its iron, 98 percent of its manganese, 72 percent of its nickel, and 61 percent of its zinc.[9] But wherever the raw materials come from, we need to remember that ultimately supply is limited. Conservation programs such as recycling are vital in making the supply last as long as possible.

5
Gardening

The Project

"God's Acre" projects, raising produce such as tomatoes, beans, strawberries, sweet corn, melons, and potatoes to sell, are traditional youth group activities. Today gardening to raise money is a better idea than ever.

Produce shipped to us over long distances burns up a great deal of energy in transport, refrigeration, and processing. Locally grown produce reduces energy consumption and is more nutritious as well.

Groups with elderly members are especially well suited for this project. After years of gardening, older folks possess valuable knowledge for producing fine harvests. They also provide built-in instructors for the younger generation.

Good planning is the key to gardening success. Several factors to keep in mind are:

(1) Choose crops with the best market potential.

(2) Line up places to sell your harvest before the crops ripen.

(3) Crops such as strawberries, raspberries, cantalopes, and beans which require a lot of labor are better suited to large groups than crops which need to be tilled or harvested by big machines.

Sometimes your project can take on more dimensions than you originally plan. A group of eastern Pennsylvania churches has started a project collecting excess garden produce, packaging it, and transporting it to the inner city. There it is sold at far below the standard market price to needy people who do not have access to low-priced, fresh produce. In 1978, the project brought in $1,100 which was contributed to a world hunger project.

As a result of the project, several youth groups are now raising crops specifically for this market. Another especially meaningful side effect is that the poor people who buy the produce feel good knowing the money they spend from their limited budgets is helping suffering people in other parts of the world. Projects similar to this one are starting up in other areas of North America.

You do not have to live way out in the country to find gardening space. There are empty lots even in some of the most densely populated cities. In many Canadian cities the parks and recreation department administers garden plots. In Philadelphia the city government gives free seeds to anyone who will garden in vacant lots.

What's the Connection?

Producing cash crops in poor countries for export to rich countries is increasingly being recognized as part of the world hunger problem. Land used for raising sugar, pineapple, coffee, and bananas can't be used by local residents to grow rice, beans, and other nutritious foods for their own consumption. And the practice is growing.

If the local population benefited from high value export crops, things might not be so bad. But they don't. Large landowners and multinational corporations reap the profits and the people are deprived of land which could be used to cultivate crops for their own use and sale.

It would seem that the writer of Proverbs might have had export cropping in mind when he wrote, "The fallow ground of the poor yields much food, but it is swept away through injustice" (Proverbs 13:23).

The amount of land used for cash crops (most of which are exported to North America, Europe, and Japan) is startling. "Worldwide, 250,000 square miles—one and one half times the area of California, enough land to feed the world's present hungry people several times over—is given over to 'cash crops' like coffee, tea, cocoa, and the rest," which may have little or no nutritional value.[10] In Central America one half of the best agricultural land is used to grow crops for export.[11]

6

Manure Gathering

The Project

Across the United States and Canada beef and dairy cattle are frequently confined in barnyards and holding pens. Often little provision is made to remove the manure. Collecting and selling the manure to city dwellers for gardens and flower beds would earn money and conserve commercial or inorganic fertilizer, which is made from petroleum.

For easiest handling, allow the manure to dry before you collect it. Then package it in used, plastic-lined fertilizer bags. The plastic liner prevents leaks and odor. A local farmer who uses fertilizer in sacks may save his empty ones for you.

Organic fertilizer customers are similar to those suggested in the firewood project. Surburban homeowners who normally purchase their manure at garden supply stores might be willing to buy from you. You won't be able to advertise that your manure is free from weed seeds like commercial varieties, but your lower price should make your product attractive enough to generate an ample profit.

An organic fertilizer project serves a number of useful purposes. First, it utilizes a valuable organic resource. Second, it helps reduce runoff and pollution problems which often arise near cattle pens. And most important of all, encouraging people to use organic fertilizer conserves inorganic fertilizer, which means saving valuable petroleum resources.

What's the Connection?

Petroleum prices, including the cost of commercial fertilizer, continue to rise as the supply of oil grows more limited. That constant spiral means that farmers in poorer countries are increasingly unable to afford the inorganic fertilizers they need. It is not surprising, then, to learn that African farmers use only one-seventeenth as much fertilizer per acre as United States farmers and a miniscule one-fortieth the amount applied to fields in Western Europe.[12]

Fertilizing soil increases the land's ability to produce crops only up to a certain point. Many European and North American farmers can no longer expect dramatic results from commercial fertilization. In poorer countries, where much less inorganic fertilizer has been used, the potential for increasing crop yield is still great—if only they could afford the fertilizer.

One hunger expert explained it this way, "As a general rule, the use of an additional ton of fertilizer in the agriculturally advanced nations will not yield more than five additional tons of grain, and in some cases much less than that. In the developing countries, an extra ton of nutrient will often produce ten extra tons of grain, and in some situations fifteen or more."[13]

7

Drying Herbs
and Teas

The Project

Climbing coffee prices and concern about caffeine and excessive amounts of salt in our diets have led many people to search for alternative beverages and seasonings. A popular beverage substitute is herbal teas. Fresh and dried herbs are good seasonings for casseroles, meats, and salads. You can capitalize on this growing market to rasie money for world hunger.

Savory, chives, parsley, thyme, oregano, basil, and many other herbs can be dried and sold. Also, an interesting variety of mints can be grown for teas. Dried herbs and teas sell best, but you may be able to market fresh potted herbs, too. Try selling them as attractively packaged Christmas specials, especially at church bazaars and farmers' markets.

Some general tips on an herb and tea project:

(1) Many herbs and seasonings are perennials which grow every year without replanting, so starting and stopping the project from year to year won't be too easy.

(2) This is an excellent family project, although a large group could come in handy for packaging and selling.

(3) Your local library should have some of the numerous good books which supply details on growing and drying herbs. *A Cook's Guide to Growing Herbs, Greens, and Aromatics* by Millie Owen (Knopf) is one of the best.

What's the Connection?

Drinking herbal beverages instead of coffee and black tea won't have much impact on the world hunger problem. But it's worth noting that a large amount of land in poor countries is devoted to coffee and tea production. For example, Brazil had five million acres worth of coffee under cultivation in 1970.

In some countries coffee is grown by small farmers on marginal land and is a valuable way for the farmer to earn extra income. Unfortunately, most of the coffee and tea shipped to us is replacing more nutritious crops like rice, beans, and corn.

Although you wouldn't guess by the number of coffee television commercials, United States consumption is declining. Just over 30 years ago, Americans drank more than 1,000 six-ounce cups of coffee per person per year. By 1976, that figure had dropped to 560 cups per person. Statistics on Canadian consumption of coffee are similar to those in the U.S.

Why the change? Higher prices and concern about how much caffeine we should consume explain part of the difference. Also, many people have started drinking other kinds of beverages, such as herb teas. For the record, U.S. tea consumption has remained close to 160 six-ounce cups per person per year for the past 60 years.[14]

8
Hunger Walks

The Project

Walks are a popular and effective way to raise money for hunger. They allow people from all age-groups and a broad spectrum of the community to participate either as walkers or walker sponsors. Walking also helps us identify with the majority of the world's people who possess practically no other means of transportation.

Although the average hunger walk covers about 10 miles in an afternoon, walkers may decide how much of the distance they want to complete. Sponsors pay a prearranged rate for every mile the walker covers.

Advance planning, with good publicity and well-prepared sponsorship forms, is essential for a successful walk. You can secure excellent help from the CROP organization. Contact your state CROP representative or write to the National CROP Office, Box 968, Elkhart, Ind. 46515. CROP walks' participants or their sponsors can choose the hunger agency to which they want their money contributed. Up to 25 percent of the funds can be set aside for local hunger projects. In Canada help can be requested from Miles for Millions, Box One Million, Station A, Toronto, Ont. M5W 1S1.

Fun variations of the hunger walk are roller skating, bicycling, and jogging events. If you select one of these options, you can extend the distance beyond 10 miles.

What's the Connection?

Walking occupies a major part of the day for people in many poor countries. Carrying produce to market and lugging water from the river or well must often be done on foot. Children walk long distances to school and adults walk to their jobs. In Nepal, Upper Volta, Pakistan, and many other countries, women and children walk several hours every day gathering cooking fuel. [15]

Gordon Hunsberger, MCC development worker, reports that the cost of public transportation also forces people to walk in his area of Northern Haiti. He says, "Many women walk the 11 miles from Bahon to Grande Riviere, carrying heavy loads, rather than pay the 30¢ fare." Walking 10 miles in an afternoon is a small, symbolic way of identifying with these less fortunate people.

9
Fasting for Hunger

The Project

What's it like to be hungry? Paul Kennel, a former Mennonite Central Committee worker in India, experimented with hunger by eating only one meal a day for a month. Afterward he wrote,

> After the fifth or sixth day I really did not get that hungry during the day, but I started to notice places to eat, and the smell of food always caught my attention. Between the second and third week, the hunger I felt was different—not the pains of hunger but a gnawing feeling along with . . . a lack of physical energy.
>
> The whole perspective of life started to narrow down. Food became a strong focus—not necessarily that I wanted to eat all the time, but that to do anything I had to have a certain amount of food. I saw things through the screen of basic human need.

As time progressed I became even more thankful for just a cup of tea or a glass of water. I saw a person begging in a completely different light. To say no to a person needing food was not done easily. I felt closely what they were feeling. I also knew that if I didn't get my one meal I would have a great difficulty doing my work. It was the same with them. Any energy expended was not from the food eaten but from oneself. It was distinctly felt.

Fasts to raise money and as an attempt to identify with those whose only choice is hunger have been used by a variety of groups. The length of the fast varies from one meal a week, to one day a week, or to an entire weekend or perhaps longer. You can fast by yourself, with your family, or with your entire group. The money you save by not eating should be contributed to world hunger. Besides raising funds, you should also gain, as Paul Kennel did, a new awareness of the importance of food in our lives and the impact an insufficient diet has on your mental and physical activity.

Fasting can also have deep religious connotations. It was practiced in both the Old and New Testament as an expression of mourning, repentance, and devotion. A well-planned fast can be a profound worship experience.

Students in college, university, or private high schools can organize a fast through the school's food service department. The business manager can calculate the amount of money saved and send it to the hunger project the students have selected. To really get a feeling of hunger, try scheduling your fast for at least two meals in a row.

While your group is fasting, you can increase your knowledge about world hunger. When you would normally be eating, try reading, discussing, or viewing films on the subject. Studying the Bible and praying can also be especially meaningful during a fast. If you plan to fast for a full weekend, Church World Service/CROP or Oxfam America ("Fast for World

Harvest") have good organizing materials (see page 70 for addresses). One word of caution: Children should not fast for more than one meal. Their physical makeup and activity requires regular nutrition. An alternative might be to have children eliminate a certain part of their meals—desserts, meat, or breads and pastries—during the period of the fast.

What's the Connection?

It's hard to say exactly how many of the world's people are hungry or starving. Estimates range from as many as one billion, that's one fourth of the population of the earth, to 450 million or about one eighth of the earth's inhabitants.

Somewhere between ten and fifteen thousand hungry people starve to death every week, many of them children. Worldwide, however, few deaths are attributed directly to starvation. What actually happens is that inadequate food weakens the body, leaving it vulnerable to numerous communicable diseases, as well as to water-borne diseases such as cholera, typhoid, and diarrhea.

Involuntary fasting is a way of life in many poor countries for several weeks or months before the harvest. After the harvest there will be food—for a while. But the food will grow scarce again before the next harvest. Unfortunately, this nutritional cutback often comes when farmers and their families need physical energy the most for planting and cultivating the new crop.

We don't need precise figures on how many tens or hundreds of millions of people are hungry to know that any number is too high. Our fasting can save food and raise money, but it can also offer us profound psychological and spiritual insights into the plight of the many people for whom daily hunger is an involuntary way of life. Perhaps those insights will lead us to even greater responses to the problem in the future.

10
House Plant
Sales

The Project

House plants are growing increasingly popular in home decorating schemes. You or your group can sell plants to raise money for world hunger. As an added benefit, local plant production conserves the energy commercial growers expend in shipping refrigerated flowers and plants long distances to market.

You'll need to spend a lot of time planning and organizing your project. Some house plants grow quickly, but others need a year or more of care before they're ready to sell. The best group for this task might be older persons or several families working together.

Several sale methods should work: yard sales, contract orders from a local supply nursery or outlet, or auctions. To add value to your plants, install them in *sikas* from Bangladesh. *Sikas* are attractive jute plant hangers available from Self-Help Crafts, a program of Mennonite Central Committee and SERRV outlets of Church World Service.

What's the Connection?

More and more of the flowers sold in North America are being grown in poorer countries and shipped north. The profits benefit only a few and it means less land is available for local food production. The authors of the book *Food First* report, "Since 1966 the value of cut flowers and foliage imported into the United States has increased over 60 times to over 20 million dollars in 1975—over 90 percent coming from Latin America.... The favored country so far is Colombia, where cut flowers are now a 17 million dollar a year business."[16]

As mentioned earlier, growing and marketing house plants saves much of the energy used to haul and refrigerate plants over long distances. If the practice caught on, it also could free some of the land in poorer countries now being used for flower production so people could grow more food.

11
Whole Grain
Sales

The Project

The difficulty many North Americans encounter in finding individual and mixed whole grains for baking and cooked cereals could become a project for you and your group. You can grind and mix the grains yourself and sell them to raise money for hunger. In addition, you would be making a contribution to better nutrition and saving energy usually burned up through commercial packaging and transportation of flours and cereal over long distances.

Grains suitable for this project include whole wheat, corn meal, rye, flax, sorghum, buckwheat, and soya. Several kinds can be mixed together and sold as cereal. You can package the grain in simple plastic or paper bags. If you hope to sell a lot of grain, you'll definitely need an electric grinder. In any case, several different hand and electric grinders are available at reasonable cost.

Many of the grains can probably be purchased locally, but be sure they're clean. If additional cleaning is required, make arrangements at a local mill or feed store. A garage or any other dry, well-ventilated building is suitable for grinding and mixing the grains. To ensure freshness, grinding and packaging should be done on a monthly or bimonthly basis. Market your product at bazaars, health food stores, farmers markets, and through "want ads."

What's the Connection?

Cereal grains hold an extremely important place in most poor countries because they make up a large percentage of the diet. In developed areas, like North America, most of the diet comes from animal products, fruits, and vegetables, rather than directly from grain. Major breakthroughs in agricultural research in the late 1960s yielded dramatic improvements in cereal grain production. Newly developed varieties of grains responded to fertilizer with 25, 50, and even 100 percent increases in the harvest. This exciting development in agriculture was dubbed the Green Revolution.

But the benefits of the Green Revolution produced some not so desirable side effects. Wheat and rice production became more profitable for large landowners. They began planting more acres of grain in place of the traditional, protein-rich legumes they once grew. The local people lost an important source of protein from their diet.

As profits grew, large landowners began pushing sharecroppers, who raised their own food, off the land, so they could till it themselves with larger equipment. To make things even worse, the new strains of grain needed more fertilizer, credit, and technical know-how. The small subsistence farmers struggled desperately and often unsuccessfully to keep pace with the march of progress.

Selling whole grain cereals won't do much to help the poor farmers of the world who are toiling to grow enough food for their families, but it can improve our own nutrition, save energy, and also provide some food for thought as we learn more about the poor and their unending battle for food.

12
Bake
Sales

The Project

Bake sales are one of the most common fund-raising projects. You can sponsor a bake sale with a difference if the items on display are made largely from whole grains. The results contribute to your fund-raising and to good nutrition. Your sale could offer breads, cookies, granola, and snack items, but should avoid the sweet, rich, heavy baked goods normally available at such events.

This is a good follow-up or partner activity to Project 11, Whole Grain Sales project. A December bake sale featuring breads, Christmas cookies, and tea rings is particularly appealing. Stress the unique purpose of your sale. This should attract some customers who don't usually patronize bake sales.

What's the Connection?

Surprisingly and tragically, many people in poor countries do not eat better when they have more money to spend on food. In fact, it often goes the other way. Why? Because many of the people prefer the white rice, white bread, highly processed foods, and soft drinks advertisers tell them people in more "developed" countries eat. Unfortunately, that more-expensive food is often less nutritious than the unpolished, un-processed food normally available for less money.

Miriam Krantz, Mennonite missionary associated with the United Mission to Nepal, has done much to help Nepali people utilize local grains and legumes to feed malnourished babies. She observed that infants often showed signs of malnourish-ment at five months of age because they were being fed polished rice and other foods from which the vitamins and minerals had been removed.

Krantz worked out a "super flour" made from soybeans, corn, and wheat or other grains available in a particular village. When roasted and ground in the traditional way, the mixture provided mothers with a relatively inexpensive porridge rich in the vitamins and minerals their children needed.

13
Fruit
Drying

The Project

Dried fruit is popular again. Bins, jars, and bags of mixed dried fruit line the aisles of many specialty shops and some grocery stores. If you live in a fruit-growing region, you can cash in on this renewed interest to raise money for world hunger. While you're at it, you'll also be conserving the energy and material needed to preserve fruit by freezing or canning.

Fruits that can easily be dried include apples, apricots, peaches, grapes/raisins, pears, and currants. In the summer of 1979 volunteers at the Mennonite Central Committee Material Aid Center in Reedley, California, dried a ton of nonsalable nectarines. The dried nectarines sell for $3 a pound. Many people turn out excellent quality dried fruit without any special treatments or preparations. But there are some tricks you can experiment with to find what works best for you.

For instance, strawberries and several other fruits can be made into fruit leathers. Coconuts become an interesting snack if you peel strips off the edge of the coconut with a potato peeler and then dry them like any other fruit. Some fruit driers brush the fruit with lemon juice or place it in a sulfur bath to keep it from turning brown.

Solar fruit driers are great energy savers. Numerous solar energy booklets now on the market illustrate several different solar drier designs.

Project 1, Gleaning, combines easily with this project. After the fruit is gathered, drying adds another way of marketing it. You can sell dried fruit in a number of ways including bazaars, through classified ads, at roadside markets, and at relief sales. Attractively packaged fruit sells well as gifts.

What's the Connection?

Our North American food system uses a tremendous amount of energy. In fact about 16 percent of the energy consumed in the United States is used to grow, process, transport, and prepare food.[17] The food industry ranks sixth among all the manufacturers.[18] Packaging frozen and processed foods uses up a great deal of energy and other scarce resources as well. In 1976, food packaging cost Americans about 26 billion dollars. That's 13 percent of their total food bill.[19]

Drying fruits and vegetables, on the other hand, requires only minimal amounts of energy and packaging. The vitamin loss in drying is only slightly less than in canned produce.

14
Thrift
Shops

The Project

In 1978, sixty Mennonite Central Committee-sponsored thrift shops in Canada and the United States earned several hundred thousand dollars selling good-quality, secondhand items along with overseas handicrafts from MCC's Self-Help Crafts Program. The profits support MCC relief and development programs in poor countries. Individual churches or groups of churches could organize a similar project to raise money for world hunger, conserve resources, and help less fortunate people in their own area acquire goods they need.

Much planning, a large group of volunteers, and a long-term commitment are the essential ingredients for a thrift shop project. A good location is also important. The most suitable items to sell are clothing, toys, tools and appliances, small furniture items, and kitchenware. A wide, well-displayed variety of materials adds appeal and improves sales. Groups interested in organizing a thrift shop should write to Mennonite Central Committee for their pamphlet, "Guidelines for Thrift Shops."

Organizing and operating a thrift shop may be a larger project than your group wants to initiate. Instead, you could organize periodic auctions or garage sales. Develop a theme for each sale—houseware, garden-lawn, children's toys, clothing, or whatever. Offer only good-quality items; customers will return to future sales if they do not have to handle three pieces of junk for every usable item.

What's the Connection?

Thrift shops are one way to get items that are normally discarded to people who have use for them. A child from a low-income family in Washington, D.C., may have only a thin winter coat. This obviously is not for lack of warm coats in the city; it is a problem of unequal distribution. Similarly, hunger is not only the result of an inadequate food supply in a poor country. Many times the food is there, but the people who are unemployed or underemployed have no money to buy it.

Worldwide tariff and trade structures are among the reasons that poor people have no work. For the most part, rich nations have slanted the trade and tariff laws to keep manufacturing and processing jobs in their own countries. They accomplish that by tacking higher tariffs on manufactured goods than they charge for raw materials. If poor countries want to make any money at all, they must sell their raw materials. When they do this, they ship away thousands of income-producing processing and manufacturing jobs too.

Cocoa is a good example of how the laws work. Cocoa beans enter the United States with no import duty. If the beans are processed into sweetened chocolate or cocoa before they arrive, a tax of 5 percent or more is placed on it. Fortunately, Canada, the United States, and several other rich countries are eliminating tariffs on more and more products from the poorest countries.

A recent book on trade says, "The annual bill paid by consumers in the industrial North for beverages, food, and manufactured goods originating in the raw materials produced by the developing world amounts to over $200 billion. Of this sum the producers of the raw materials get only $30 billion. . . . If more of the processing could be shifted to the Third World it could gain as much as $150 billion in annual earnings."[20]

If our trade and tariff structures were changed, jobs could open up for thousands of people in poor countries. The money those people earned would create an even more important result. With it, hungry people could buy life-sustaining food.

15

Feeding Another Person

The Project

North American families are smaller today than they were a generation ago. Most families could afford to feed more children, but they have chosen not to. A good family project is to contribute to world hunger the amount it would cost to feed another person in your family.

Calculating the cost of feeding another mouth can be done in a variety of ways. If your family keeps a close record of food expenses, some quick division should yield the amount of money you spend monthly on each family member. You can donate that sum weekly or monthly. If you don't have your own figures to work with, you can use the United States Labor Department's periodic statistics on the cost of feeding a family of four. In Canada consult Statistics Canada, an arm of the Ministry of Industry, Trade, and Commerce.

Families can dramatize this project in several different ways. For instance, you could set a place for the "new" child at your table, or you could decide as a family which country or specific project you want to support. Interest your family by allowing one of your children to help fill out the monthly or weekly contribution check and by studying the culture and dietary habits of your imaginary family member.

What's the Connection?

Your "feed another person" project may help in a small way to offset the growing impact large multinational companies are having on the dietary habits of people in poor countries. The damage is being done because poor people are responding to advertising which is designed to sell products to middle- and upper-class people in the same country.

Baby formula companies, for example, have aggressively promoted their products through billboards, milk nurses, radio, and TV. The advertising convinced many impoverished mothers that bottle feeding is better than breast feeding. Tragically, when these mothers switched to what they thought was a more beneficial method, unsanitary conditions, impure water, and a lack of money to buy enough formula combined to produce a higher death rate for bottle-fed babies than for those nursed the traditional way.

In response to public outcry, most companies claim they have discontinued the worst abuses in infant formula advertising. But the problem continues because of earlier and some current promotion of formula as the modern and desirable way to feed a baby.

For more information on the infant formula situation, contact: Interfaith Center of Corporate Responsibility, 475

Riverside Drive, Room 566, New York, N.Y. 10027; INFACT, 1701 University Avenue S.E., Minneapolis, Minn. 55414; IN-FACT Canada, 1611 Quadra Street, Victoria, B.C. V8W 2L5; or your denominational hunger concerns office.

16
Export Crop Surcharge

The Project

A quick glance at your pantry shelves or down any local supermarket aisle should reveal to you how many of the foods we eat are grown in poorer countries. As the number increases, the U.S. and Canadian food systems are gaining a reputation as global supermarkets. Foods we consume in massive quantities like cocoa, sugar, pineapples, bananas, lots of winter vegetables, watermelons, and strawberries come to us from places like the Dominican Republic, Colombia, and Mexico.

While the amount of food shipped to us is high, the wages poor people receive for growing it are very low. These low wages are a major reason why imported crops can compete with those locally grown. Improving the situation of sugarcane cutters and banana pickers is a complex task. Project 5, Gardening, describes the economic consequences producing crops for export has for hungry people in poor countries.

One way you or your group can identify with poorly paid workers in other countries is to place a voluntary surcharge on certain imported crops. Twenty-five or 50 percent of the price you pay for the food is about right. Your action will serve as recognition that these imported goods should cost more than we normally pay for them. Depositing your surcharge money in a simple container after every shopping trip will remind parents and children that great injustice exists between the rich and poor countries. Try to contribute the money you accumulate to an agency which is working at the root causes of social and economic inequities.

Mennonite Central Committee and many other denominational mission and service agencies work at root causes of hunger in addition to providing emergency relief. They also attempt to identify and witness to the United States and Canadian governments about policies that affect the poor. Another Christian agency that specifically addresses public policy issues of world hunger is Bread for the World. Arthur Simon, Director of Bread for the World, said, "Each year Congress routinely chops about $200 million or more from . . . development aid. Thus, in one vote Congress can wipe out the value of all contributions for church relief agencies for an entire year."

What's the Connection?

Charging ourselves more for the imported foods and minerals we consume can help us develop an understanding of the economic structures which rich countries have built at the expense of poorer nations. To combat the inequality which now exists, those poor countries have begun calling for a New International Economic Order. They want higher prices for the goods they sell to wealthy nations, more stable prices, and more control over production, shipping, and marketing.

Bananas are a good example of how things stand now. If you look at the produce counter of your grocery store, you'll find that bananas usually cost less per pound than apples, even though the bananas were shipped thousands of miles and the apples were grown nearby. The fact that more perishable bananas must be transported from field to store more quickly than apples doesn't seem to affect the price.

A United Nations report on export crops showed that, on the average, only 11¢ of every dollar we pay for bananas stays in the country where the fruit is grown.[21] The rest is swallowed up by foreign corporations which control the production, distribution, and marketing of the bananas. No one has calculated what part of the 11¢ left in the country goes to the people who pick the fruit and haul it to the ships.

17
Junk Food Surcharge

The Project

Most of us experience a twinge of guilt when we eat our favorite "junk food," probably with good reason. Soft drinks, chips, candy, and many other snack foods may be affecting our health adversely with their loads of chemicals, fat, sugar, and salt. Plus they are expensive, overpackaged, and replace more nutritious foods in our diet.

To reduce, or entirely eliminate junk food from your diet, you or your group could charge yourselves double the price of snack foods and contribute the extra money to world hunger. Voluntarily inflating the price will show you just how much of these foods you're eating. Chances are you'll cut down on them while you're raising money.

What's the Connection?

Not everyone in North America enjoys the eating standard you and I do. Seven percent of the United States' population receive public assistance payments which do not provide adequate resources for the people who get them. Fifty-four percent of poor North Americans are children under 18 and elderly people over 65.[22]

Fortunately, food stamps and other domestic food aid programs are helping. A 1977 report says fewer people in this country are grossly malnourished today than 10 years ago. According to the report,

> This change does not appear to be due to an overall improvement in living standards or to a decrease in joblessness in those areas. In fact, the facts of life for Americans living in poverty remain as dark or darker than they were ten years ago. But in the area of food there is a difference. The food stamp program, the nutritional component of Head Start, school lunch and breakfast programs, and to a lesser extent the women-infant-children (WIC) feeding programs have made the difference.[23]

18
Saving
Gasoline

The Project

In their great love affair with the automobile, North Americans do a lot of unnecessary driving. You or your family could set a goal to reduce your driving and contribute the money that would have been spent on gas to world hunger.

First, decide how much driving you want to eliminate. Ten to twenty percent less than the last couple of years is a good start. Then try some of these suggestions:

(1) Don't use the car for trips less than a mile unless the weather is bad or you need to transport something heavy.

(2) Keep a "town list" to coordinate your errands and allow you to accomplish more things in fewer trips.

(3) Observe driverless Sundays like some European coun-

tries have been doing since the 1974 oil embargo.

(4) Choose some other weekday on which you will not use your car.

(5) Develop the habit of thinking whether the trip is needed before you get into the car.

Individuals and families can do well with this project, but youth groups could also covenant together to reduce their total driving by a predetermined amount. Periodic reporting sessions will encourage members to keep working toward the goal. The money collected for the miles not driven can be given to a hunger project as a group contribution. Not driving will be easier if your group brainstorms a little to discover less energy consumptive forms of recreation and entertainment.

What's the Connection?

Transportation is the second highest energy consumer in the United States. The fuel-use pie splits up this way: industrial, 41.2 percent; transportation, 25.2 percent; residential, 19.2 percent; and commercial, 14.4 percent. Cars alone burn up 13 percent of our total energy consumption.[24] A Hertz Corporation study shows that owning and operating a car or truck in the United States soaked up more than one quarter of the national personal income in 1978. Using a 4,000 lb. car as a grocery wagon is the least efficient link in the food chain.

Reducing the amount of driving we do will directly affect the world's limited petroleum supply. Keeping the supply as abundant as possible means the price may well be lower for purchasers in poor countries. It also means there may be more left for generations of earth citizens still to come.

19
Weight-Consciousness Clubs

The Project

One-third of North America's population is at least 10 pounds overweight. Take a look around next time you attend a sports event or church picnic or while you're waiting on a street corner. You'll be shocked at what you see. Our diet habits and inactive lifestyle are causing us problems.

Many overweight people are joining groups which help them lose unwanted pounds. The key to such groups is the affirmation and encouragement members give each other to keep working toward their goal. Church or community groups could form their own weight-consciousness clubs with the special rule of contributing money to world hunger for each pound of weight lost.

Overweight people are often self-conscious about their fat and have difficulty getting rid of it. They need affirmation, not the criticism many slimmer people are tempted to give them. A weight-consciousness club can be a good way for people to start losing weight and it can provide long-term encouragement after the initial enthusiasm fades. Groups should meet every week or two to sustain their momentum.

What's the Connection?

Americans eat much differently today than they did 70 years ago. One of the biggest changes has been increased sugar and fat consumption because we are getting our carbohydrates from different sources.

In 1909, 56 percent of our carbohydrates came from flour and cereals while 22 percent came from sugar and sweeteners. In 1976, cereals furnished only 35 percent of our carbohydrates, while 37 percent came from sugars. Fat consumption climbed 28 percent between 1909 and 1976. Fresh fruit and vegetable consumption dropped during the same period.[25]

Dietary changes like these, coupled with our less active lifestyle, are contributing to increases in diabetes, heart attacks, strokes, and tooth decay. Changing our eating habits can improve our health. And, if we're really serious about it, we can raise a significant amount of money for world hunger, too.

20
Eating-Out
Clubs

The Project

Driving from 25 to 50 miles to try out a new restaurant is not unusual today. Many people spend significant sums of money searching for convenience, great food variety, or a unique dining atmosphere. But spending for one meal what a Christian brother or sister in a poor country earns in a month is unjust. The amount of food wasted in some restaurants is a problem, too. An eating-out club, with from three to six couples or individuals involved, provides a variety of meals and decor, raises money for world hunger, and offers good fellowship which is probably the most rewarding part of eating together anyway.

Club members agree to take turns preparing and hosting an elegant but simple meal in their homes instead of visiting a restaurant. Everyone who participates, except the host, contributes to world hunger the amount of money they would have spent if they had eaten the meal in a commercial establishment. Rotating the meal preparation prevents anyone from bearing an undue burden in cost and work. Basic guidelines should probably be established to avoid the development of a "one-upmanship" syndrome.

What's the Connection?

Increased eating out, particularly in fast-food establishments, has contributed to the North American diet changes described in Project 19. Currently, one out of every three American food dollars is spent away from home, mostly in restaurants. By 1990, that figure is expected to rise to 50¢ out of every food dollar. We need to recognize that our extravagant lifestyle is helping neither our own health nor the plight of the poorer people in other parts of the world.

21
Sprouting
Seeds

The Project

Sprouts have been an important part of the East Asian diet for centuries. In recent years people have begun growing sprouts in America and Canada, especially when fresh garden produce is not available for winter salads. Grocery stores in the Western parts of the U.S. and Canada usually sell fresh sprouts, but stores in the Eastern section of both countries often do not. Your group can meet the sprout demand and raise money for world hunger.

All you need to get started is a warm place, water, and quart- or gallon-size wide-mouth jars. Mung beans and alfalfa sprouts are the most commonly used seeds. Sprouting takes three to five days. All you need to do is rinse your crop daily. If you're a beginning sprout grower, consult your library for books with more detailed instructions.

You can arrange standing orders with friends and neighbors to sell your sprouts, use classified ads, or market them through local health and grocery stores. You might want to keep sprouts growing all the time or you can start them periodically and inform your customers of your production schedule.

What's the Connection?

Sprout growing won't have much impact on world hunger, but the simplicity of producing them contrasts sharply with the rest of the North American food system which uses much more energy than food production and distribution systems in other countries. Tractors, combines, and other farm machinery used in the actual growing of food burn about 3 percent of all motor fuel used in the United States.[26] The entire food system, from seed to supermarket, consumes 12 percent of U.S. fuel, with food processing demanding twice as much energy as farming itself.[27]

With its energy-intensive nature, the U.S. farming method could never be exported intact to other countries, especially poor ones. If you tried it, you'd use up 80 percent of the world's annual energy supply just to feed people.[28]

Growing sprouts meets a produce demand without using the energy normally expended in shipping refrigerated goods long distances. Hopefully, it will also make us more sensitive to the amount of the world's energy we demand to sustain our affluent, North American lifestyle.

Notes

1. Sterling Wortman and Ralph Cummings, Jr. *To Feed This World* (Baltimore: Johns Hopkins University Press, 1978), pp. 77-79.

2. "Food Ecology: A New Idea for Changing the Food Waste Culture" (Food Ecology Center, P.O. Box Drawer 1435, Atlanta, Georgia 30301).

3. Robert L. Loftness, *Energy Handbook* (New York: Van Nostrand Reinhold Co., 1978), p. 162.

4. *Ibid.*, p. 124.

5. Denis Hayes, *Repairs, Reuse, Recycling—First Steps Towards a Sustainable Society* (Washington, D.C.: Worldwatch Institute, Worldwatch Paper #23, September 1978), p. 29.

6. *Ibid.*, p. 5.

7. E. J. Kelly, District Manager of Reynolds Recycling Co., as quoted in the November 4, 1978, issue of *Lancaster Farming*, Lancaster, Pa., p. 128.

8. Hayes, *op. cit.*, p. 17.

9. Martin M. McLaughlin, *The United States and World Development, Agenda 1979* (New York: Praeger Publishers, 1979), p. 192.

10. Colin Tudge, *The Famine Business* (New York: St. Martin's Press, 1977), p. 7.

11. Ronald J. Sider, *Christ and Violence* (Scottdale, Pa.: Herald Press, 1979), p. 69.

12. Wortman and Cummings, *op cit.*, p. 67.

13. Lester Brown, *By Bread Alone* (New York: Praeger Publishing Co., 1974), pp. 118-19.

14. Letitia Brewster and Michael Jacobson, *The Changing American Diet* (Washington, D.C.: Center for Science in the Public Interest, 1978), p. 18.

15. Eric Eckholm, *The Other Energy Crisis: Firewood* (Washington, D.C.: Worldwatch Institute, Worldwatch Paper #1, September 1975), p. 5.

16. Frances Moore Lappé and Joseph Collins, *Food First: Beyond the Myth of Scarcity* (Boston: Houghton Mifflin Co., 1977), p. 266.

17. Anne Barrett Pierotti and Albert J. Fritsch, *Lifestyle Index-77.* (Washington, D.C.: Center for Science in the Public Interest, 1977), p. 13.

18. *Ibid.*, p. 15.

19. Brewster and Jacobson, *op. cit.*, p. 2.

20. Philip Land, "Impact of Trade and Debt on the Developing Countries," *Growth with Equity: Strategies for Meeting Human Needs*, by Mary Evelyn Jegen and Charles K. Wilber, eds (New York: Paulist Press, 1978), p. 179.

21. Lappé and Collins, *op. cit.*, p. 194.

22. Mariellen Procopio and Fredrick J. Perella, Jr., *Poverty Profile, U.S.A.* (Paulist Press, New York, 1976), p. 42.

23. Nick Kotz, "Feeding the Hungry," *The New Republic*, November 25, 1978.

24. Loftness, *op. cit.*, p. 158.

25. Brewster and Jacobson, *op. cit.*, pp. 56, 62.

26. "Agricultural Energy: Getting Your Fuel Tanks in Perspective," *Successful Farming*, May, 1975, p. 20.

27. Denis Hayes, *Energy: The Case for Conservation* (Washington, D.C.: Worldwatch Institute, Worldwatch Paper #4, January 1976), p. 42.

28. John S. Steinhart and Carol E. Steinhart, "Energy Use in the U.S. Food System," *Science*, April, 1974.

Additional Resources

Books

Brewster, Letitia and Michael F. Jacobson. *The Changing American Diet*. Center for Science in the Public Interest, Washington, D.C., 1978.

Brown, Lester R. *The Twenty-ninth Day: Accommodating Human Needs and Numbers to the Earth's Resources*. Worldwatch Institute/Norton, New York, 1978.

Hunt, Linda, *et al.*, *Loaves and Fishes*. Herald Press, 1980.

Jegen, Mary Evelyn and Charles K. Wilber, *Growth with Equity: Strategies for Meeting Human Needs*. Paulist Press, 1979.

Lappé, Frances Moore and Joseph Collins. *Food First: Beyond the Myth of Scarcity*. Houghton Mifflin, 1977.

Longacre, Doris Janzen. *Living More with Less*. Herald Press, 1980.

_____. *More-with-Less Cookbook*. Herald Press, 1976.

McGinnis, James B. *Bread & Justice: Toward a New International Economic Order*, 1979.

Mitchell, Don. *The Politics of Food*. James Lorimer and Co., Toronto, Ontario, 1975.

Perelman, Michael, *Farming for Profit in a Hungry World: Capital and the Crisis in Agriculture*. Allanheld, Osmun & Co., Montclair, N.J., 1977.

Rifkin, Jeremy with Ted Howard. *The Emerging Order*. Putnam's, New York, 1979.

Shoemaker, Dennis E. *The Global Connection: Local Action for World Justice*. Friendship Press, 1977.

Sider, Ronald J. *Rich Christians in an Age of Hunger: A Biblical Study*. InterVarsity Press, 1977.

Simon, Arthur. *Bread for the World*. Eerdmans, 1975.

Taylor, John V. "Enough Is Enough," reprinted from the *Church Missionary Society Newsletter*, London, England, September 1972.

Van Beilen, Aileen. *Hunger Awareness Dinners*. Herald Press, 1978.

68

Audiovisuals

Bangladesh Plowman. Available from MCC, AV Library, 21 South 12th St., Akron, Pa. 17501. 22 minute color film. Also available from MCC provincial and regional offices.

Bread and Justice. Produced by Peace and Justice Institute. Available from MCC, AV Library, 21 S. 12th St., Akron, PA 17501. 3 filmstrips each 20 minutes, color, 1979.

Collision Course. Available from MCC, AV Library, 21 S. 12th St., Akron, Pa. 17501. 45 minutes, color film.

Food First. Produced by Institute for Food and Development Policy. Available from MCC, AV Library, 21 S. 12th St., Akron, PA 17501. 2 filmstrips each 15 minutes, color, 1979.

Give Us Daily Bread. Available from MCC, AV Library. Also available from MCC provincial and regional offices. 23 minutes, 16mm color film.

Guess Who's Coming to Breakfast. Available from MCC, AV Library, 19 minutes, color filmstrip, 1977.

Hamburger USA. Produced by American Friends Service Committee (AFSC). Available from Mennonite Central Committee, 21 S. 12th St., Akron, Pa. 17501. Also available from MCC Central States Region, 106 W. 24th St., N. Newton, Kan. 67117; Millindo food and hunger offices, Rt. 2, Box 79, N. Manchester, Ind. 46962; and the AFSC, 2160 Lake St., San Francisco, Calif. 94121. 28 minutes, color, slide-tape show.

People's Technology. Available from MCC AV Library, 21 South 12th St., Akron, Pa. 17501. Also available from MCC provincial and regional offices. 17 minutes, color filmstrip, 1978.

Promised Land Lost. Produced by MCC and Eastern Mennonite Board of Missions and Charities. Available from MCC regional and provincial offices and Eastern Mennonite Board of Missions and Charities, Salunga, Pa.. 17538. 20 minutes, color filmstrip with study guide, 1979.

Sharing Global Resources. Available from MCC, AV Library; and American Friends Service Committee, 2160 Lake St., San Francisco, Calif. 94121. 35 minutes, color filmstrip, 1977.

A World Hungry. Available from MCC, AV Library; and Franciscan Communications Center, 1229 S. Santee St., Los Angeles, Calif. 90015. 5 filmstrips each about 12 minutes, color, 1975.

Agencies Involved in Relief and Development Programs

American Friends Service
Committee (AFSC)
1501 Cherry St.
Philadelphia, PA 19102

Catholic Relief Services (CRS)
350 Fifth Avenue
New York, NY 10001

Christian Reformed World Relief
Committee
2850 Kalamazoo S.E.
Grand Rapids, MI 49560

Church World Service/CROP
Box 968
Elkhart, IN 46515

Lutheran World Relief (LWR)
360 Park Avenue South
New York, NY 10010

Mennonite Central Committee (MCC)
Box M
Akron, PA 17501

MCC (Canada)
201-1485 Pembina Highway
Winnipeg, Manitoba R3T 2C8

Oxfam America
302 Columbus Ave.
Boston, MA 02116

Oxfam of Canada
97 Eglinton Ave. East
Toronto, Ontario M4P 1H4

United Methodist Committee for
Overseas Relief (UMCOR)
475 Riverside Dr.
New York, NY 10027

World Neighbors
5116 N. Portland Ave.
Oklahoma City, OK 73112

World Relief Commission (WRC)
P.O. Box WRC
Wheaton, IL 60187

World Vision International
Box O
Pasadena, CA 91109

Paul Longacre has had wide experience in relief and development work. He, along with his family, served with the Mennonite Central Committee (MCC) in Vietnam and Indonesia. He also served in various administrative assignments in the MCC headquarters office in Akron, Pennsylvania. Most recently his responsibilities are providing information on world hunger issues for the North American churches. He has served as a speaker and workshop leader on numerous occasions in both the United States and Canada. His articles on world hunger subjects have appeared in Mennonite and Brethren in Christ periodicals.

He worked closely with his wife, Doris, in compiling and writing the *More-with-Less Cookbook* and *Living More with Less.* Upon her death in November 1979, he carried primary responsibility in bringing the latter book to completion.

He is a member of the Akron Mennonite Church, serving as an elder with responsibility for finance and stewardship. He also serves as chairman of the Overseas Committee of the Mennonite Board of Missions in Elkhart, Indiana.

He is father of two daughters, Cara and Marta, ages 14 and 12, and currently resides at Akron, Pennsylvania. He graduated from Goshen College, Goshen Biblical Seminary, and Kansas State University.

ADDITIONAL HUNGER RESOURCES FROM HERALD PRESS

More-with-Less Cookbook
by Doris Janzen Longacre

Over 500 recipes that allow you to eat better while consuming less of the world's food resources. "The message of this book is appealing: Simplify your diet. Although the basic premise of the book is an effort to waste less of the world's resources, the inescapable side effect is that we also spend less at the checkout counter."—*Chicago Tribune*

Over 350,000 in print.

Living More with Less
by Doris Janzen Longacre

Practical suggestions on living with less contained in chapters on clothing, housing, transportation and travel, eating together, housekeeping, recreation, money, meetinghouses, celebrations, and strengthening each other. "If you feel discouraged or alone in your pilgrimage towards simple living, if you have heard enough theory and want practical, concrete suggestions, if you are ready for a challenge, read on. In this unique volume of personal testimonies woven together by superbly written, thought-provoking introductions, Doris Longacre offers an excellent combination of theory and practice."—Ronald J. Sider, author of *Rich Christians in an Age of Hunger*

Hunger Awareness Dinners
by Aileen Van Beilen

Three types of hunger awareness dinners provide different approaches to the hunger problem. They teach facts about calorie and protein intake, and about the amount of energy used in growing and processing food around the world. "The dinners are an excellent way for congregations to become aware of the enormity of the world hunger challenge and the part they can play in alleviating it."—*World Encounter*

HERALD PRESS
Scottdale, PA 15683
Kitchener, ON   N2G 4M5